Dropshipping:

Guide for E-Commerce Business. The Explanation of a Model for Beginners to This Online Job, Including the Marketing Strategies.

Table of Contents

Introduction

Dropshipping is a supply chain technique that allows an individual to earn money by acting as the middleman between a supplier and a customer. The retailer lists products for sale and the customer will place an order with the ecommerce store. The payment for this product (sold at a markup) is sent to the account of the retailer, and the order and shipping information is received in the retailer's email. The retailer then forwards this order and mailing information to the supplier and pays the supplier for the product and shipping using the customer's money. The products are prepared and shipped directly to the customer. The retailer didn't have to purchase any inventory, pay to store the products, or bother with shipping out the orders.

If you want to make money with drop-shipping, you'll need the right niche for your store and the right collection of products to offer. To find a successful niche, look at the best-selling categories on Amazon. When starting out, sell products that are already popular in that niche. Then, as your store's customer base grows you can include other products. If you don't wish to pick a niche, you can run a general store. This allows you to incorporate a variety of products and you won't need to worry about being able to incorporate a specific item into the theme of your store. The benefit of a niche store, however, is that it allows you to build a reputation, or brand, within your niche and this reliability can translate into a more loyal customer base.

To sell these products, you'll need a website to serve as a store. This can be created using WordPress or a Shopify theme even if you have no coding experience, You can easily outsource this step to a professional. This store will be your business headquarters, so it needs to be neat, professional, and easy to navigate. Your website's domain name should be the same as your store name, so take this into consideration when naming your store. The products should be listed with multiple professional looking images and keyword heavy product descriptions.

Drop-shipping is one of the cheapest ways to open an online business because it doesn't require investing in any inventory. You can start a drop-shipping store for less than $100, but turning that store into a passive income stream will require investment in outsourcing and automation.

There are also some downsides to drop-shipping. The products you are selling are representing you, but you don't really get much control over what that representation looks like. Your store has no choice over packaging or presentation, although some suppliers might let you customize these things for a fee. Because you are the face of the product and the retail process, you are also held responsible if anything goes wrong with the product or the shipping. You'll have to be the liaison between the customer and the supplier, which is one of the reasons it's very important to choose the right supplier. You also have to go through the supplier if you need to contact the shipping company, which can be frustrating and time consuming. Over all, there are risks involved but drop-shipping can be a great introduction to online business and can provide a buildable source of passive income.

What is dropshipping?

Dropshipping is a business model where there is no need to maintain inventory, own a warehouse, store goods or even directly ship products to the customer. This is all done by a third-party called a supplier. The store owner simply makes the products available for purchase to customers at a marked-up price. Then, the seller forwards the customer information to the supplier, along with payment, when an order is made. The seller keeps the profit.

The start-up cost of running such a business is very low and as such dropshipping is something that new entrepreneurs commonly turn to. Most business owners in this model fall under the millennial and Gen Z category. There are many advantages to the dropshipper, including being able to set their own prices and the huge profit margins that are possible. Profit margins usually fall between the 35% and 45% range for the luxury item niche and can go even above 100% for items like jewelry and electronics. In fact, the common advice by the professional dropshippers is that products should be marked-up no less than 300%. The niche that the dropshipper decides to sell in can have a huge impact on the profit margin so it is something that you should consider carefully if this is a business model that you plan to pursue.

How Dropshipping Works

The first process that happens in the dropshipping business model is that the dropshipper enters into a partnership with a supplier who manufactures or stocks, warehouses, packages and ships the product to the customer when an order is made. The dropshipper then lists this product on a website such as an ecommerce store and promotes the produce and website to drive traffic and potential customers to that store. Those potential customers view the items, and if interested place an order.

After the order has been made, the dropshipper manually or automatically forwards the details of the customer to the supplier undersupply of packages who ships that item directly to the customer in the dropshippers name. This is a very neat and tidy process and simplified it looks like this:

1. A customer views and purchases the product that has been listed by the dropshipper at the price that it has been listed.

2. The order is forwarded by the dropshipper manually or automatically to the supplier and the dropshipper pays the supplier.

3. The supplier ships the product directed to the customer and the dropshipper's business name is listed on the packaging.

Dropshipping Myths

Before we get into the nitty gritty of setting up your own dropshipping business, let's discuss dropshipping myths you may have encountered in your search for more information concerning this business model. Are they true or false? Let's find out!

1. You can only dropship from the US or to the US. This myth is definitely false. As a dropshipper, can ship to anywhere in the world and can operate from anywhere in the world. Most people focus on the US simply because it has hundreds of millions of potential

customers who welcome the convenience of the ecommerce industry and are willing to buy.

2. It can take several weeks and even months for customers to receive dropshipping items. This is both true and false. How long it takes a customer to receive an item depends on their location in the world relative to where that item was sourced from. Therefore, if the customer is close in relation to the supplier then he or she will receive this item quicker than someone who is a lot further away. This is an eventuality that a dropshipper should anticipate and should have countermeasures to ensure that all of his or her customers are happy with the delivery of products.

3. Dropshipping is easy. This myth is false - initially. I say that because it takes quite a bit of upfront work to make a dropshipping business successful but once the groundwork has been laid out, it becomes a lot easier to manage.

4. Customers do not buy from new dropshipping stores. That is false. Just as you have given a brick-and-mortar store a try simply because a product interested you or the brand resonated with you, online consumers patronize new ecommerce stores all the time. The key

to attracting new customers to your ecommerce store lies in the effectiveness of your marketing.

5. The dropshipping market is oversaturated and dead. This myth is definitely false. The dropshipping business model has been around for a long time and there is a reason for its longevity; and that is because it is so effective.

Chapter 1: Pros and Cons of Dropshipping

Pros of dropshipping

The immense growth in the dropshipping market clearly points hands to its numerous benefits. Some of the benefits of dropshipping are shortly outlined.

No start up capital – Perhaps the major reason why dropshipping is really a trending business is that merchants do not need to have any capital to venture into it. Traditional retailing requires you to invest possibly thousands of dollars in upfront inventory but dropshipping allows you to start up the business without any capital. This is made possible because you purchase products from merchants with the same money paid by consumers. You would have made the sales before making the purchase, this makes dropshipping to appear as a win-win business model and lucrative for start-ups.

Easy to expand – You are not limited to a single supplier in dropshipping, you can get your products from as many suppliers as possible. This allows you to expand your niche and offerings and to offer better products and services to your customers. Since the suppliers handle the shipping process, the dropshipper has all the time he requires to focus on the main aspects of his business and marketing. This makes it easy for the dropshipper to have the time required to scale the business and incorporate other products. To scale the business, the dropshipper mostly require an efficiently working and robust website that can attract a large number of customers. Of course, the business becomes more complex when it is expanded but since the merchant does not cater for the shipping process and product delivery, he can focus on the integral parts of the business no matter how complex.

Easy to commence – The entry barrier to the dropshipping market is very low because it is very easy to start. Since the dropshipper does not deal with the shipping and stocking, inventory and warehouse fees, and managing the stock level, it is relatively easy and less complex than a traditional brick to mortar kind of business. Put together, the merchant in a dropshipping business makes relatively low overall expenses when compared to his counterparts in brick and mortar retailing. He can even run the entire dropshipping business from home and will spend the low amount of money on the facilities to stay online. Of course, the cost and requirements of dropshipping increase as the business grows and scales but they are still low in comparison to brick and mortar retailing.

Cons of dropshipping

The benefits of dropshipping make it a very tempting venture; however, you might want to weigh both the merits and demerits before venturing into it. Some of the downsides of dropshipping are shortly discussed.

Complex logistics as the business scales - Dropshipping logistics could become very complex as the business expands. Most merchants in dropshipping have more than one supplier and the suppliers themselves rely on several warehouses to provide the goods. This can make it very difficult to manage the inventory and can mar the customer services. Failure to adequately and effectively manage the logistics can result to ineffectiveness in the product tracking system, delays in shipping and so forth which will ultimately lead to poor customer experiences. While there are some systems to enhance logistics and inventory, some of the systems may not really deliver the effectiveness required in logistics management.

Low entry barrier – This appears to be a benefit but in actual sense, it is a demerit. Since it is easy to start up a dropshipping business and it requires no capital, virtually anyone can setup his own business. This means high competition, low margins, and some other demerits. Low margins could particularly be worrisome. The merchant may decide to reduce his product costs to a very low amount in order to attract customers but at the end of the day, the customer services may suffer direly. Since the suppliers are up for business, they can as well drop ship for anyone else as well as you. This makes the competition really tense and stiff.

Lack of uniqueness – Everybody wants to drop ship. This makes uniqueness really an issue in the dropshipping market. Most of the merchant's products are sold by some other merchants out there and customers can easily find a competitor to buy from. However, dropshippers go to extreme length to look for really unique products but since it is a very open market, the products will soon lose their uniqueness because some other dropshippers will start selling them.

Chapter 2: Dropshipping ebay, Amazon and shopify

How to Dropship on Amazon & eBay

If instead of creating your own website, you want to dropship on an existing platform or marketplace, Amazon and eBay should be among your top considerations. Let's discuss how you can set up your dropshipping store on these two marketplaces.

Amazon

Being the biggest name in retail e-commerce, Amazon has a lot of inherent advantages as a dropshipping platform. You can open a dropshipping account with Amazon and take advantage of their market share and stellar reputation to sell your products. Amazon buys products from suppliers in bulk, so they have massive inventory in warehouses in different parts of the world, which means that if you work with them, your small shop could grow fast and operate globally.

With Amazon, you also have access to a large market of more than 300 million users, which means that you could get large returns if you have great products and strategies. Because Amazon already has hundreds of millions of potential customers, you don't have to spend too much on advertising. In fact, you can easily advertise within the platform itself. If you optimize your page, you could get organic traffic there without needing to advertise.

Before you choose Amazon for your dropshipping platform, you should understand that they have one major downside. They prioritize merchants who use their FBA program over those who dropship with the help of third-party suppliers. If you are using Amazon's FBA program, you actually have to buy your inventory upfront and send it to Amazon's warehouses where it will be stored until it's shipped out to customers. If you wanted to limit your startup costs to almost zero, the FBA program probably isn't your best option, so stick with dropshipping. That being said, Amazon is a great place for drop-shippers because it has some of the best shipping times and quality control measures in the whole retail e-commerce business.

Many people think that dropshipping is against Amazon's terms of service, but it's actually not. Amazon doesn't allow arbitrage dropshipping (this is where people source products that are cheaper from places like Walmart and eBay and then sell them through Amazon). Amazon allows private third-party fulfillment of customer orders, as long as it's your business name that appears on all the purchase and shipping slips that are attached to the product. According to the Amazon TOS, you have to be the "seller of record," which means that if you use a competitor of Amazon's (like Target or Walmart), they may close your account.

Here is how to go about dropshipping on Amazon:

First, you should get a professional Amazon seller account. You should pay the fee for a pro account because the free account will limit your ability to grow and scale once you have started your dropshipping business. There are also certain categories in Amazon's platform in which you cannot sell products if your account is a free one.

You also need to get UPC codes (Universal Product Codes) for all your products. There are lots of services online that can help you acquire UPC codes, so with a little internet research, you can easily figure out how that works. You also need to get suppliers, and they shouldn't be big box suppliers (big companies that compete with Amazon in the retail market).

Use a product research tool to find a great product to sell on Amazon. Remember that with Amazon, it's even much harder to compete in popular niches because there are other sellers who have been around longer and they have positive reviews, so you have to go an extra mile in your product research.

You also need enough capital to sustain your business in the first few months because it takes a while for Amazon to pay its merchants, so you can't count on the payout from your sales to maintain cash flow.

Also, make sure that your suppliers ship the products pretty fast (preferably within 5 business days). That's because Amazon customers are accustomed to fast shipping, and the platform keeps metrics of its drop-shippers which customers can see. If your metrics are poor, customers won't be too keen on buying from you. Amazon is a bit strict when it comes to quality control, and if you get a high number of product returns or cancelations, or if your metrics are terrible, they could suspend you from their platform.

As a drop-shipper on Amazon, the way you create and organize your listings will determine how many sales you will be able to make. First, to increase your chances of success, make sure that you have lots of product listings on your account. Second, you have to be well organized in the way you list your products. Make sure that you use bold and clear titles and descriptions that sound like professional sales copy. You should also use high-quality product images for all items in your listings. As a drop-shipper, you may not be able to use PPC ads for your products because Amazon prioritizes FBA merchants over drop-shippers, so your best chance of boosting your visibility is by optimizing your product pages.

You should be careful when selecting the products to dropship on Amazon because not all products are suited to be drop-shipped on this platform. You should choose a niche where people are passionate and very specific about the products, which means that they will be willing to wait a little longer to receive that particular product. If you go to a niche where products are readily available everywhere else, you may not be able to compete with merchants who use FBA, mostly because of their faster shipping times.

Most Amazon drop-shippers eventually end up switching over to the FBA program. They use dropshipping to test the viability of a product in the market, and then if it works well, they switch to FBA to take advantage of Amazon's fast shipping, advertising, and other perks. If you have the capital, you can adapt this model to increase your competitiveness within the Amazon platform. If you would rather stick with dropshipping, you may be able to offer incentives to your customers to make them more willing to wait for a little longer for their packages. You can add a small freebie to every product that your customers purchase to entice them to select your products despite the longer shipping times.

Finally, when shipping with Amazon, be extremely careful about copyright and trademark issues because you could get authenticity claims from big companies, and Amazon could shut your down. Otherwise, Amazon is a great place to run a dropshipping business, and all you have to do to succeed there is to work smart and hard and follow the rules.

eBay

eBay is a great platform for dropshipping mostly because it adds a twist to the dropshipping model. Instead of just having a fixed price for your products, you can set up auctions for each listed item (especially if the products you are selling are rare and high-value items). It's also less restrictive when it comes to the kind of products that you can sell. Unlike Amazon, you don't have to worry too much about where you source your products, as long as you are able to deliver.

eBay is like the wild west of online retail because it allows people to sell all sorts of new and used items, so if you want to stand out and gain the trust of customers, you should be able to provide as much information about yourself and your product as you can and try to make your listings look professional. Compared to other platforms where you can start your dropshipping business, eBay is probably the cheapest because it doesn't charge any fees (like Shopify and Amazon).

To start dropshipping on eBay, go to their website and open an account. You can either open a personal or a business account, that doesn't matter since most dropshipping functions can be performed by both accounts, plus you may be able to upgrade a personal account into a business one if the need arises. The account opening process is fairly standard. You just have to fill in your personal information and contact information, and towards the end of the process, you will need to add a PayPal account to your eBay account. After signing up, you can personalize your account by adding a logo. The whole process should take you less than ten minutes if you have all your details ready.

When you start selling on eBay, you will only be allowed to list a few items at a go (about 10 items). As you make more sales, the platform will increase your limit more and more. You have to write good product descriptions with eye-catching titles for your products, indicate their prices, and then use high-quality images to show the product from multiple angles. eBay listings differ slightly from listing on personal websites or other platforms because you have to add terms of sales and shipping information within the description for each product.

For each product that you list on eBay, you have to go through the same listing process since eBay doesn't support synchronized settings across multiple listings. If you exceed your listing allowance, eBay might charge you a listing fee for the extra products. eBay listings usually expire after thirty days, so if you want yours to stay up beyond that period, you have to go to 'setting details' and set your preferred duration for that listing. The "Good till canceled" option ensures that your product stays on the site until you decide otherwise.

You will then input the price, quantity of items, payment options, buyer privacy setting, sales tax for the product, and your preferred return options. When it comes to returning options, you have to choose the length of the return window for the product, and the action that you will have to take when dealing with returns. If you feel like your customers could benefit from some further explanation of your return policy, there is a field where you can insert additional information.

You will then have to fill in all your shipping details. You can select different shipping options for different regions. You should also specify your shipping method, fees, durations, etc. You will then click the "list" button to publish your listing on eBay. In case you have left an important detail out, eBay will notify you and allow you to fix the error.

After you have listed your product, you could start promoting it on social media platforms almost immediately to drive traffic to your page. When you make sells, you will contact your supplier and have him ship the product to your customer within your stipulated time period.

Shopify

Shopify is by far the best online tool for drop-shippers who don't have the technical expertise to create their own shops. It makes it possible for anyone to sign up and start his own online store in just a few minutes. It's great for people who want to start a dropshipping business but lack the technical know-how or the resources to build their own e-commerce websites from scratch. If you want a hassle-free experience as you start your first store, you should seriously consider using Shopify. The service offers free trial periods for beginners who want to test the waters before making a financial commitment. Here is a step by step guide to help you start your first Shopify dropshipping store.

Choose a Name for Your Dropshipping Store

When creating a Shopify store, your first task will be to select a name for your dropshipping business. You want to make sure that the name you select is simple, creative, and memorable. If you already have a niche in mind, you could try to find a name that is related to that niche so that people can have an easy time figuring out what you are selling. There are some online business name generators that you could use to come up with a list of possible names before you narrow it down to one.

When you find a few possible names that you may want to use, you must check to see if they are available. Google each of your shortlisted business names to see if they are already in use. If you use obvious sounding names such as "American Watches," chances are someone has already thought of that, and they are already trading under that business name, so try to think outside the box.

Create a New Shopify Account

Shopify has made this step extremely easy. All you have to do is go to the Shopify homepage. At that page, you will find a field where you have to enter your email address to start the process. Once you have entered the address, click the "get started" button. You will then be asked to create a password and input your chosen store name. Shopify will ask you a few questions about how much experience you have had in the e-commerce sector, and then they will ask you to provide a few accurate personal details. After you are done providing those details, your account will be officially opened, and you can then proceed to optimize your settings.

Set Up Your Account and Add All Necessary Information

You have to go through your new account's settings one menu item at a time, and you are going to input the information you need to configure your account before it can be operational. You have to put in place the correct settings to allow you to receive customer payments, to create your shipping rates, and to establish your store policies.

When customizing your account, your first task will be to add one or more payment options to your store. Unless you have this in place, there will be no way for your customers to pay you for the products they'll purchase. Go to your Shopify settings page and click on the tab that has the word "payment" on it. You will have the option to add a PayPal account or to use other payment solutions.

We highly recommend that you use PayPal because it's extremely convenient and it has a deep market penetration, so most people who shop online already have PayPal accounts of their own. You can also opt for other payment systems if you find them convenient or necessary given the particular nature of your products (for example, if yours is a store that mostly sells products to offices and other businesses, you may find it more convenient to add a payment system that allows for bank transfers.

After you have all your payment channels in place, it's time to set your store policies. These policies will govern the relationship between you and your customers, so you should make sure that they are clearly stated and that they are compliant with the law.

Shopify understands exactly what kind of policies you might need for your store, so they have created a tool that enables you to automatically generate store policies that are standardized. You can immediately generate a refund policy, a privacy policy, and even a set of terms and conditions that will protect your store from legal liability in many foreseeable situations. To gain access to the policy creation tool, you have to click on the "checkout" tab, the go through the page to find each of the fields that you have to fill. You can then click on the "generate" button, and your policy will be set.

When your customers check out after making a purchase, the full text of the policy will appear, and they'll have to accept those terms and conditions before the sale goes through. If you have your own conditions that you want to include in the policy, there are some templates that you can use as guides to create your own policy.

Finally, you will have to declare your shipping rates. Many e-commerce experts recommend that you should account for the shipping price when you mark up the price of each item in the store, and then, you should offer your customers "free shipping." This is a marketing technique that works pretty well because it makes most customers believe that they are getting a great deal, so they'll be more inclined to go through with the purchase. You can click on the 'Shipping' button and select your preferred shipping options for different zones, starting with domestic ones and proceeding all the way to international zones.

Launch Your Dropshipping Store

After you are done with your settings and configurations, you should proceed to launch your new dropshipping store. To do this, click on the "sales channels" option, and then click on "Add sales channel." When you are done with that step, you will have a real online business that is up and running.

Design and Personalize Your Store

Now that you own an online store, it's time to personalize it. Here, you have to consider how you want your customers to view your site as they browse through it and make purchases. The design of your shop is going to be crucial, and it may have a huge bearing on your level of success as a drop-shipper. You want to make a good first impression when customers visit your site, and you want to project an image of professionalism. The two most important design aspects that you have to consider are the theme and the logo of your shop.

Shopify has a large collection of themes in their inbuilt theme store, so you don't have to worry about finding a theme that suits your brand. You can use a free theme option, or you can pay a little money for a premium theme. If you are working under a tight budget, a free theme will do just fine. However, if you are very particular about your branding, you may want to go for a premium theme. Try out a few themes before you settle on one. After selecting a theme, you can customize it to make it more reflective of your brand.

Logos are important for branding purposes because they enable customers to remember your dropshipping store in case they want to make more purchases in the future. Your logo should blend with other design aspects of your shop because you want to create a sense of uniformity.

You can use tools like the Oberlo Logo Maker to create a high-quality logo in a matter of minutes. All you have to do is play around with colors, fonts, and icons. If you are a skilled graphics designer, you can create your own logo and upload it onto your Shopify account. You can also hire graphic design experts for cheap on sites like Fiverr and Upwork. After you are done with both the logo and the design of your store, it's time to add your products.

Add Products to Your Store

To add a product to your shop, go to Shopify Admin and click on "Products." You should then click on the "Add a Product" button on the top right part of the page.

You will then have access to fields where you can enter the title and the description of your product. Fill the fields by either copying and pasting the text from your supplier's website or adding a description that you have prepared on your own. Make sure that you use colorful language in your product description because your customers are going to make purchase decisions based on that description.

You should then scroll down the page and find the "Images" section. Here, you have the option of adding images by uploading image files from your computer. You can also use "drag and drop" to achieve the same outcome. Make sure you upload your favorite product image first because it's the one that is going to act as a "featured image," meaning that it will appear prominently on the sales page when your customers scroll through your shop.

You should then review all your product details, particularly the "visibility" settings to make sure that your product is set to appear on the online store. You should also review the "Organization" settings and modify them to make sure your product is properly categorized according to Vendor, Product Type, and Collections.

You then have to input the price of the product. As you do that, you can select an option that makes it possible for customers to compare prices, and you can also check a box that allows a tax to be added to the final price of the product.

When you get to the inventory section, you should add your SKU, your Inventory Policy, and a Barcode. Indicate whether or not your product has a shipping price, then select the weight bracket of the product. If your product comes in different sizes and colors, you should fill the "Variants" section appropriately, and put in the different prices for each variant.

Finally, you should edit your Meta Title and Meta Description in order to improve your SEO (search engine optimization) so that customers will have an easier time finding your product online. Ensure that you save all your product information correctly and that you view your product listing from the front end to see it from the point of view of the customer. You should repeat all these steps to add more products, or you can use services such as Oberlo which can help you add products to your account automatically.

Start Selling and Cashing in

Now that everything is done, you can start making sales. Remember that dropshipping is a competitive business, so you should do everything that you can to promote your products on blogs, social media, and other websites. Advertising is also an option if you have the resources.

Chapter 3: Tools That You Need for Your Store

In this rapidly changing world, no business can survive without using certain online tools. These provide assurance to the business when trends change and act as a backbone whenever any support is required. The convenience that using an online tool provides is incomparable to other manual forms. Whether it is making calculations for inventory or to make business expansion plans, technology plays the biggest and most significant role. Productivity and efficiency have increased by a lot, especially in the past decade as businesses of all sizes have had the opportunity to update its online services. The constant need to be updated with changing technology is essential for businesses to be able to attract new customers with ease.

Creating your e-commerce store

To explore the potential of your store, you need to be ready to adapt to all the available platforms, which will ensure the sustainability of your business. Before even looking all of the options available to make your store stand out, creating an e-commerce store is the first step. It is a necessity to have sound knowledge in technology and the online tools that are out there to start. There are professionals who can set the store up for you, as well as websites solely dedicated to help out beginners like you. Do not hesitate to seek help! These platforms are very well suited to e-commerce entrepreneurs who are just starting out. Moreover, these applications can guide you through steps to manage almost everything when launching your store.

Picking a theme

Now comes the part where you need to focus on particular and intricate details of your niche that will define your e-commerce store. However, before this step, you need to have good knowledge of the type of products you want to work with. The very inspiration for having a relevant theme that portrays your vision comes from your product range. If you are seeking help from a professional website or application, you will find a lot of preset themes there already. These can help you in brainstorming ideas and making decisions if you are unsure where to start. More importantly, think about customizing your store and giving it a unique touch. In a lot of cases, generic designs can be a turn off to consumers, while innovative ones can entice high-end customers and turn them into returning customers in the long run.

Designing an e-commerce store

Whenever customers visit your store, the theme, color palette and the design are the first things that they notice. At times, you may wonder, "Why do I need to put an extra effort into making it pretty?" or "Isn't having a great range of products enough?" Well, the answer is simple - if consumers are not interested, they will not bother going through whatever your store has to offer. Having an aesthetically pleasing e-commerce store entices customers and also validates your business as a professional one. With word of mouth, more people can become aware of and take notice of your store. If it is unorganized or shabby, it would be very difficult for you to attract them. Hence, to have and maintain loyal and potential customers, investing your resources on building a good e-commerce store is a necessity.

Online Logo Makers

After you have designed and set your store up, now is the time to brand it. This helps to gain recognition for your products and creates a lasting first impression in the minds of the customers. It can be anything from a simple tree to an intricate design; this should depend on the type of products you are selling. It is better to be more open to ideas and new designs instead of being adamant on one. Having a professional store can do wonders and help create a buzz among customers. Hence, a logo is the simplest and best solution for you to put your business out there. If you want to experiment, do not shy away from creating your own design but if you are not proficient enough, do not shy away from help from online logo makers. Hiring graphic designers or outsourcing can be great options too, depending on the budget you have for creating the logo.

Payment processing

Due to globalization, we have access to faster services, much faster than those in the past. The systems for making online payments have developed immensely and have made it easier for us to make daily purchases. You do not need to carry cash around all the time. Their personal information and details are encrypted and have protection from credit card frauds for when businesses are willing to adopt such models. You should do research on the most common online methods of making payment among your targeted customers and make sure that you provide them with those payment services. PayPal is one of the most efficient systems in the most recent times. You can also be open towards offline payment services but the online payment methods are much more convenient in today's time.

Online business plan services

If you are happy with your strategies and find that they are working for your business, this should not be a tool you need. However, it is recommended that you explore these services. An outside perspective is necessary for you to be able to work on your shortcomings. For entrepreneurs, these online plans for your business guide you in designing a feasible and strong plan when you are making the transition from great idea to a profitable business venture. The inbuilt features and tool templates of web based applications help you generate charts on performance and goal achievement. Your financial status, depending on investments made for the business, can be studied carefully. You can be in charge of and keep track of the progress that you are making. Once you learn about what the services offer you, it would not be a surprise to see that you have started to think more critically and that your ideas for your store and product line go beyond the surface.

Using social media for your store

Whether you want to focus on Facebook, Instagram, Twitter, or any other social networking website, engagement with your customers through this platform is one of the most effective ways to draw and drive traffic to your store. Using social media is attractive as you do not have to invest a lot of money into it and you can utilize it to broaden your reach. Millions of people all around the world can engage with your store. Specialized tools on individual platforms are available to make social media users aware of new products and you have the flexibility to promote your products and content related to them. This also helps you to create a brand for your store. The best part is that as more time passes by, these platforms continue to grow and once you can get comfortable with social media, you should expect to look at great numbers!

Web hosting

The pace of the business world is much faster than what it was ten years ago. You cannot expect to apply those same strategies for attracting customers today. Hence, if you have not explored the internet yet, you will lag behind and before you realize, you will already be out of the game. A web hosting service allows you to start a website and run it. The files that makeup the website on a data server can be stored through these services and these files are uploaded to the web automatically from your web hosting service. The use of email marketing and installation of one-click supported applications are some of the many features that you can use when building your business. You can also be assigned an email address that includes the site's domain name.

Shopping cart software

When you have set up your website, there are some additional things which you need to offer your customers when they make a purchase. Shopping cart software is necessary to be able to make payments through your website. This is not only beneficial for the customers as it can allow them to feel safe when buying something online, but it is an advantage for your store too. Tracking inventory gets easier and you can keep tabs on which product to promote or communicate with the suppliers if a surge is predicted with the latest trends. This will also help you produce reports based on this data through your website's services. This software can be connected to multiple platforms for making payments. PayPal or credit card services can be offered to customers and this makes their experience more familiar as well. The purchasers can also be aware of the amount of tax they are paying and how much they are being charged for shipping costs. You promote transparency and convenience through these services on your store's website and it will help you gain a good reputation among old and new customers.

Webinar services

As your business grows, you may think of expanding and gaining new customers, both locally and internationally. Webinar services can help you connect and take orders faster and most importantly, they can help you monitor your day to day operations, especially if you have multiple offices. This will help you out if your employees are working remotely and if you have multiple working locations. Training sessions, meetings with all of your employees, either within a specific branch or all together, can be conducted much more comfortably. Webinar services are a great fit for you when you want to present your sales online and make product demonstrations for your clients too. Becoming more proficient in this helps you connect with your customers faster and you can respond to their queries in real time.

Anti-virus software

When you are using your computer, it is highly likely that you are storing information through a variety of applications. Whether you are dealing with storing personal information or you are processing orders, you need to keep all the data in an organized way. The information stored here is valuable and not having any protection programs on your computer puts you and your business in a lot of danger. Apart from the technical issues that your computer will go through, you could experience data theft, which would be a very big loss for your business venture. All businesses should have anti-virus software to guard the computer network against viruses, malware, Trojans, worms, or spyware. Since the platform of dropshipping is online where you have to constantly be in touch with your suppliers and customers, having a good antivirus software is a necessity and it is equally necessary for protection.

Receiving payments from customers

In order to deal with customers from various backgrounds, your knowledge in different modes of payment platforms is required. It reduces hassle if you can connect to multiple platforms that your customers will feel safe using. There are additional charges when you want to use these online payment platforms, ensuring to keep you safe against business fraud. You will be charged a fee for every sale you make and an additional amount to ensure protection for your store. You should check out different platforms apart from PayPal to make a sound decision, however, it is and has been the most trusted and convenient one in the market. Apart from this, there are built-in features to provide you protection if you are using platforms like Shopify.

Online data storage

Due to the ease of an online platform, storing data has become much easier than it used to be. Online data storage acts as backup storage if anything goes wrong with your computer. Of course, you can access your data online even if no problems arise instead of relying on your computer's storage. Data is stored on a cloud server which is convenient and safe. You can access the files from any part of the world at any time. Also, if you want to free up space on your computer, having online data storage is the best way to go about this. It is wiser to have online storage as hard drive failures, theft, and file erasure can occur and make these files extremely difficult to retrieve.

Business tools that you should know how to use

Google AdWords & Analytics

Google is the place we think of going instantly whenever there is something we want to know. From getting instant information about the most complicated technologies to doing the most basic spell checks, Google is our one-stop solution. For your business, you need to learn to make the most of this platform. Whenever you want to know about anything, this search engine can give you around 40,000 results per second and is definitely the most reliable search engine today. You can focus on getting on the first page of the search list and witness how this changes your income. Use an SEO (search engine optimization) strategy to try and make it on the first page. It may take a long time, maybe even months or longer, but you should keep at it. This will ensure you benefits in the long term. However, there is another way that can help you attain a first-page position faster, and this strategy includes using Google AdWords. This is a scheme of paid ads where you pay every time a visitor clicks on your advertisement. Additionally, you need to invest time into how to utilize Google Analytics and understand its importance for your website and your business. This tool allows you to understand the types of mediums through which your visitors come from and this could be a huge advantage when you are starting out or are struggling to reinvent your line. Overall, this will assist with things that are working and not working, guiding you towards better execution and expansion plans.

SurveyMonkey

Now that you have set your store up and are getting ready to attract customers to your niche, you need to know about the current market and what the trends are. This is a surveying tool available online that helps you connect with your audience. Survey Monkey already has a lot of preset questions along with built-in templates to give you a thorough insight when analyzing data. The best aspect is that the tool gives unbiased responses which can help you modify your strategies or help you create new and improved ones. The free version of this tool still provides you a lot of information through the surveys but the number of features is limited. Give it a try and see how much it helps improve your product line. If you are finding it useful, go ahead and get a subscription with a paid plan. The paid plan will provide many more useful tools for surveying.

X-Cart

For newcomers who do not have a lot of money to start out but want to give dropshipping a shot, your e-commerce website still needs to stand out. This tool is cost-effective and will not put a strain on your funds. X-Cart has a free version if you want to give it a try and see whether you find it suitable for your business or not. It helps you build your website and you can explore its various features. Moreover, free extensions will allow you to create shipping labels, slideshows, and do so much more! Your business can access these facilities and prioritize what will be more beneficial to get started on in terms of harnessing technical skills. You can get acquainted with the different themes available online and customize them wherever you feel necessary.

Tableau Public

This is a marketing tool that helps you to conduct research and lets you make a thorough analysis of your business data. You learn to make better predictions on what will work and what will not and this helps you make better decisions for the future. This tool is very effective because it sources out data from CSV files and Excel among many others. When the business venture is new, investing in high profile marketing research tools is important but expensive. This is where this tool is handiest as it can give free access to up to 15 million rows in one workbook and provide data solutions for free with up to 10 gigabytes of space.

BuzzSumo

In the modern day, social media has been the best platform for marketing. Social media is perfect for if you want to understand demographics, connect with influencers, find out what the most shared content is and much more. BuzzSumo is the best influencer marketing tool that allows you to find out what content is performing the best on any social media platform. You can choose a paid subscription but there is a free trial period too which you should definitely make use of before making a purchase. This application helps you understand what sort of content will work well with your product line; this in turn will help you connect with influencers who can help you in expanding your marketing strategies.

Designhill

Lack of personalization during the shipment process, executed by your suppliers can make it difficult for your customers to relate with your brand. In such a scenario, you can simply add your logo to the package; this will help you promote your brand. Through Designhill, you can access countless templates for free and it even helps you create your own brand name. You can insert your store's name and pick themes, colors, icons to match your niche. You can choose a logo from the app's generated logos and purchase it to obtain the copyright. You can spend according to your budget and get started with this graphic design platform. The platform is powered by AI and allows you to design a logo on the go.

These tools should give you an idea about the factors that are important for you to be updated on to run your business smoothly. You should focus on your niche and work around it with the insight of technology. Since technology improves every day, it is useful to become proficient at using these applications as you gain more experience through your dropshipping store. It will help you explore better solutions to your needs and gain technical expertise accordingly.

Chapter 4: Niche Research

Product research is critical to the success of your business. You must select a great product if you want to create a business that will help you earn more than 100k per month. To select the perfect product for your dropshipping business, you need to spend some time on research.

There are three important things that you need to keep in mind while selecting a product for your dropshipping business. The product that you opt for needs to be profitable, it needs to have good demand, and it must be easy to ship. If the product that you opt for meets all three requirements, then you are off to a good start. Research is a critical aspect while you are searching for the best dropshipping products for your business. You need to immerse yourself in the virtual world of online businesses, go through different marketplaces like eBay, Amazon or AliExpress. You need to understand the product trends, the sellers who are active in a given niche, the profit margins, seller fees, and the shipping costs. If you already have a list of potential products that you can use for your dropshipping business, then you can test them with the criterion that is discussed in this chapter.

Brainstorm

If you have a list of products that you think will be good for your dropshipping business, then that's great. If you don't, then you don't have to worry.

It might seem like a basic step, but it is quite important. When you are thinking about all the different products that you can dropship, you might start to wonder if a specific product might sell online. You need to make a list of all the products that you think will sell online. At times these ideas might pop into your mind when you are thinking about a product that might solve a problem you are facing in your life. You can also get product ideas when you interact with others. Before you can select a great dropshipping product, you need to take some time and think about all the different ideas for products that might be floating around in your head. Even if the idea seems ridiculous initially, please make a list of the product ideas. You must also acquaint yourself with the products that are doing well on different marketplaces.

Google Trends

Google trends is an fantastic tool for having an understanding of what is popular in the moment. Taking advantage of this gives your products much greater exposure and a greater chance of being purchase while the trend plays out. Disadvantages of following trends is of course the lifespan of your products. This however plays into the advantages of dropshipping, allowing you to effectively grow your business in peak times while trends are hot and then changing direction when business starts to slow down. All the while not having to move and manage large quantities of inventory which can be painful after a particular trend has dried up. The best way to help you learn is to provide examples. Please look carefully.

You will arrive at this page when you go to www.google.com/trends/ Type in the search bar whatever product you are interested in selling or think that there is high demand for. It can be anything, do not be afraid to be creative. Anything can be sold online nowadays. However try to be alittle sensible and logical about it. Think about the shipping costs involved and the viability of the product. For example, no one in the right mind would purchase a refrigerator online. It is a strong retail product that requires the customer to touch and feel before making a buying decision. Furthermore, the shipping cost required to send a refrigerator from China to your customer would eat up a huge chunk of your profit margin, if anyone would purchase from you online in the first place. Hence it is recommended to think of a product that is relatively small, constantly in demand and is economical with regards to the shipping costs and your profit margin. In the first example we are going to use the word "bicycle" and determine if it is a good product to sell based on our search result on Google Trends.

Do you think that a bicycle would be a good product to sell online based on the result above? The graph tells us that there is a decreasing number of searches for the word "bicycle" over the years. This is what we call a "sunset" product. The trend is dying and the product is in low demand. Less people have searched for that word on Google in recent years. Now we shall use another example to show how powerful Google Trends can be in determining if your product idea is in demand and can actually be very profitable for you.

We have used the words "Korean cosmetics" in the search this time. As you can see, there is a distinct uptrend in the number of searches especially in recent years. This is a good sign as it signifies that this product is in the growth stages. More searches for this keyword means there is more demand. It is increasing over the years. This graph is a great example of a healthy product in the stages of expansion and growth in awareness. There is increased interest over time. This might spell an opportunity for you.

Social Shopping Websites

There are different social shopping websites or online marketplaces that are curated by not just users but even the tastemakers. They are quite helpful since they list the products that appeal to online shoppers. It will also help you gain insight into the kind of products that are trending and are popular before they become mainstream. These websites will save you time and you don't have to go through the thousands of product lists on your supplier's websites or other platforms like eBay or Amazon. Instead they offer a curated list of items based on current trends in the market. A couple of places that you can visit to gather this information are wanelo.co/stores, fancy.com/shop, wish.com, and etsy.com.

e-Commerce Stores

When you are thinking about the different products that you can dropship, it helps to learn from those dropshippers who are doing well in the field. You can look at the different products that the successful e-commerce stores are selling. Make a note of their listings, the photography, and the sales copy they use. All this can act as inspiration and help you come up with product ideas of your own. Going through the websites of your competitors will also help you visualize how your online store will look.

Retail Price

The price at which you can sell the product for is known as retail price. Ideally, as a dropshipper, you must opt for products that can be retailed for anywhere between $15 and $200. It might sound like quite a margin between these two numbers, but it is considered something of a sweet spot if you are interested in dropshipping. There are multiple reasons why the best dropshipping products retail for this price range and they include the following:

If you are selling a product that is perceived as being affordable, then it is quite likely that you will be able to sell high volumes of such a product. If you can sell high volumes of a product, then it increases the chances of obtaining customer feedback. Customer feedback is critical when you are building your credibility as a dropshipper. If you sell the products for less than $15, then it will significantly lower your profit margins and you will need to sell a lot of stock. On the other hand, if the product retails for over $200, then it is not considered to be affordable and it can be quite difficult to sell. Also, if you sell products for more than $200, then when you need to make any refunds, it can really burn a hole in your pocket.

So, does that mean that you can never sell over $200 per product? Well, the only time you can go higher than $150 is when you are able to sell the products with a minimum advertised price or a minimum retail price (MRP). If a product has an MRP, it means that you cannot sell the product for a price that's less than the MRP set by the manufacturer. For instance, Apple has a strict MRP policy on their products and no retailer can offer a better deal on iPhones than any of its competitors in the market. Opting for MRP products is a good idea because it prevents dropshippers from competing on the price and, instead, they need to focus on the value addition and the benefits they can offer customers. If you are just getting started with dropshipping, then it is a good idea to stick to this price limit.

Recommended Margin

The product that you want to dropship needs to offer a profit margin of at least 20-40%. The profit margin of a dropshipper is usually higher since sellers have the option to markup their retail price by 100% or even more. If you are dropshipping a product that retails for $200, then you can have a profit margin of up to 30% on such a product and you will be left with a profit of about $60 per order. If you decide to sell a product that retails for $20, then you must increase your profit margin on such a product. Remember that while you are setting your margin on the product you want to dropship, there are a couple of things that you need to take into account like packaging costs, shipping charges, marketing costs, and any other expenses that you might incur while making a sale. Therefore, it is always a good idea to opt for a product that offers a high-profit margin.

Weight and Size

Ideally, the best products for dropshipping are those that can easily fit into a shoebox. Anything larger than that and it will increase your shipping costs. You need to be mindful of the weight and size of the product if you want to be a successful dropshipper. The profit margin of your product will decrease considerably if you have a very high shipping cost. Most dropshippers tend to use ePacket as their shipping partner. ePacket is a shipping service that allows the users to quickly ship products from China or Hong Kong to the United States and over 30 other countries. If you want to use a shipping service like ePacket, you must be mindful of the size and the weight of the products. ePacket has a minimum and a maximum weight requirement for the products they ship. If you want to take up dropshipping, then you must look for products that are small, weigh less, and are easy to ship.

Moving Parts

An ideal product for dropshipping is one in which little can go wrong. You must avoid products that are fragile or fiddly, since they can easily break while being shipped and it will result in a lot of negative feedback from customers. Electrical gadgets fall into this category, especially if you are working with an unfamiliar supplier. It is a good idea to stick to products that are sturdy and can sustain the international shipping process.

Potential Repeat Business

One criterion that a lot of new dropshippers forget is that a great product means repeat business. It means that if the product is something that the customer likes, then it is quite likely that such a customer will be potentially a repeat buyer. A new concept that has become quite popular these days is the idea of subscription services. There are businesses that offer everything from luxury chocolates to feminine hygiene products that are delivered monthly to subscribers. This gives the seller a predictable monthly business. The ideal categories for this sort of business model are the products that fall into the category of health and beauty products that a person needs to purchase every time they run out. If you can successfully convert a customer, then the chances of repeat business increase, so try to check for products that you can use for a subscription service.

Supplier

Selecting the product is as important as selecting the right supplier for your dropshipping business. Without a good supplier, you cannot fulfill your orders on time and it will not help you with your business. As a dropshipper, you will potentially rely on the supplier to manufacture the product, maintain sufficient inventory, and ship it to the customer in a timely fashion. You will learn more about selecting a supplier in the coming chapters.

Low Turnover

The product that you want to dropship must be something that will stay in production constantly. If you want to dropship a product, then you will need to invest in good quality photographs and sales copy for the product listings. If you opt for a product that will stay in production at any given time, then you can make your investment in photography and the likes last you longer. Products with a high turnover (the products that get discontinued quickly or change every couple of months) are not a good option since you will need to constantly spend money to upgrade and revamp the website and your product list.

Trials

This is an exciting step while selecting a product. If you have a dropshipping idea that made it through the previous steps and it seems like a good idea, then you need to think about whether the product will work or not. A product might look great on paper, but it needs to do well in real life as well, so the best way to test a product is to order it for a trial. It helps to test the quality of the product and the efficiency of the supplier as well.

Chapter 5: Product Selection and Preference

As of this point, we have understood what drop shipping is, its benefit and shortcomings. Then we moved on to the supply chain and fulfillment process, understood that then saw how to start and run your business. We shall now take a look at the key factors before settling for a product. You need to consider a lot and it is not straightforward. Also realize that for flow and understanding, this chapter had to come sixth, however, product selection essentially should be one of the first things you should consider,

Here are some key pointers:

- **Sole pricing and distributions:** If it is possible for a manufacturer to enable you to have exclusive pricing and distribution of a product then this places you several cuts above the rest. However, such agreements are very hard to come by but in the event that you can pull a few strings, nothing illegal or unethical, then this will highly favor you.

- **Offer the lowest prices:** Of course. If you can offer a product at a price lower than everyone else's then you'll totally blow away the completion. Only one problem though, this model WILL fail, eventually. Giants such as Amazon will eventually catch wind of this and the last thing you want is to get into pricing wars with those big boys. Therefore, low prices are only good while they last.

- **Offer non-priced value:** For instance, along with the product you sell, offer supplementary information that complements the product. This very simple tip adds a lot of value to a simple product without the client incurring any extra expenses. Do not just sell a product, sell solutions.

- **Great images:** The first interaction between a client and a product is through images on your website. Ensure that the images are of impeccable quality. Check out sites like Burst for free high definition product photos.

- **Components:** The more components a product has the more components a client will be required to buy. You could sell furniture, but that's it, one of the desks is sold, the end. Or, you could sell home theatre systems that have dozens of components and require wiring.

- **Accessories and customization:** In the same line as components, think of products that can be customized and/or may need complementing accessories. A very basic rule of engagement is, lower priced items such as accessories should yield much higher margins. For instance, a laptop may yield a 3% margin but its skin may yield up to 200%.

Simple human behavior dictates that we are much more cautious about spending big but care very little about 'cheap' purchases which may not be cheap at all. For instance, when shopping for a phone, we shall carefully weigh our options and after a short while to think eventually settle for one and will grab a good looking case from the same store without really considering the price.

- **Size:** Go small. Shipping large and/or heavy items will be stressful, cumbersome and not to mention costly!

- **Impossible to find locally:** Market research will do you a world of good when it comes to this. Do not sell products that people could find at literally any corner of the neighborhood. Find out what it is people want and cannot seem to find locally.

- **Marketing potential:** Let's face it, is impossible to market some products. You would not want to be a couple of months into your business and realize that you cannot acquire customers because your range of products is not marketable.

Types of Customers

Customers are human beings. You will come across an insane variation of customer behavioral tendencies. But the one we find the most intriguing is when customers who spend the least complain the most and those that spend ungodly amounts are usually very laid back. However, this statement is very subjective and does not cut across everyone. Also, we do not wish to sound discriminative against those that spend less. The funny bit is that smaller items actually have larger margins thus making us the most profit. Then, from that perspective, doesn't that essentially make small spenders our largest income generators? If yes, then maybe they do have a right to complain.

Understanding and settling for the right demographic are key towards making it big. Here are some groups of people you could tap into.

- **Hobbyists**: Some people are mad obsessed about what they do in their free time, a concept we human call hobbies. These people would spend ungodly sums of money to facilitate their hobbies. Some hobbies include hiking and some sports. We even know of mountain bikers who have bicycle more expensive than their cars. This is a lovely niche to tap into since they are willing to spend. In a later chapter, we shall see how important specialization is. Do your market research and find out what people in your target market like to do. For example, if you live in a mountainous region, you could specialize with hiking gear.

- **Businesses**: Business would be amazing to work with for two reasons, they seek competitive prices which you offer and they buy in bulk which makes them suited to work with drop shippers. All you need to do is offer impeccable customer service, which we shall also cover in a later chapter, consistency and you will go into their books as their default contact person whenever they need something.

- **Repeat Buyers** – Only but as few things in life can be compared to the bliss of receiving recurring income and this is one thing repeat buyers offer.

The one way to attract repeat buyers is to work with either hobbyists or/and businesses as we have highlighted. But there also a way to tap into the regular customer. Offer products that will constantly require re-ordering, have a short life span, are disposable, need accessories and or customization and those that will need technical support. This will ensure that the client will always come back to ask for something else. Oh, sweet cash!

There are three concepts we shall not get into but are very vital in regard to this section. As much as we have put out across a criterion that will very much likely act as a guide towards selecting products that will yield the highest returns, there are three other things you need to consider before you do so: **Trends, demand,** and **competition**. These three factors will play a very vital role in the success of your business.

Demand: Is the product you seek to push in demand? Yes it might meet all the point in the criteria but people might simply not want it. Yes, it might be marketable or it might have a million components that go with it but it just might not be in demand!

Trends: This one is bitter-sweet. Why? Investing in trends can work out and it also can be disastrously bad. This is because some trends pop up and stay for eons while others disappear as soon as we heard of them Human intuition and judgment shall be called upon here. Try and study trends and find out whether they will leave any meaningful mark on this world or a quick pastime.

Competition: Do we really need to expound on this one? You need to realize that you are not the only one in this business. Too much completion means that the field is crowded and starting out, you will struggle to generate traffic and build a client base, too little competition, however, is an indicator of a small market.

Fortunately, Google is very effective at analyzing all three. The Google keyword tool is very effective at analyzing both trend and demand, and as of competition, we shall highlight later on why Search Engine Optimization would be key to beat this.

Chapter 6: How to find suppliers for your dropshipping

Now that you have a general idea of how to decide what type of products to sell (your niche), how to start a website, and the basic procedures involved with dropshipping through your wholesale suppliers, it's time to actually begin looking for suppliers.

Find Your Suppliers

There's an almost infinite amount of choices when it comes to wholesalers that will make dropshipping a possibility for you. That doesn't mean you should just throw some darts and work with whoever it lands on. On the contrary, it means you need to take time to decide which providers can offer the most for you. Finding the ones that can provide great products for your niche can be difficult sometimes, and it means taking quite a bit of time to determine which sources are truly the best.

Since dropshipping doesn't refer to a specific service or business, it can really be any business that sells products. The obvious thing here is that we are going to avoid retailers. There are no profits to be made paying full or close to full price and trying to resell. There are too many costs involved to make this practical. Wholesalers are a great source of lower prices and good services, but manufacturers that will ship for you directly may be able to offer you the absolute best prices.

Remember, some of these suppliers that specifically advertise as dropshippers are going to be less-than-reputable and should be avoided. Here are the signs that you should steer clear:

• Monthly fees... very few legitimate suppliers chare a specific monthly fee.

• Anyone can buy... on the other hand, you should have to be a member. Places that sell products on a retail site are probably not a great dropshipping solution. They may not be a scam, but they aren't often giving you prices that you can work with.

• They have poor ratings on consumer sites like the Better Business Bureau, Yelp, Google Businesses, etc. Always check your supplier's reputation online before engaging in any business with them. You have too much work to complete to waste time on shady suppliers.

The unfortunate truth is that many wholesalers aren't especially happy to work with first-time sellers. It can easily be a big waste of their time, and for this reason, they often require that an initial order is going to be at least $500, sometimes more. For these situations, if you really want to work with the wholesaler, you should offer to deposit $500 to them in exchange for credit that can be spent as you begin making sales. Alternatively, you can establish your business a bit more and return to these sources. They will be more likely to allow you to skip the initial order if you can demonstrate that you're a serious business entity.

Locating these suppliers is possible through many methods:

• Directly contact manufacturers. Most manufacturers are not in the business of selling one or two items at a time, and that means that you may have an impossible time working with them directly unless you can offer them large amounts of business. However, it is still often worth contacting the manufacturers that whose products you would like to purchase. Instead of asking for them to allow you to send orders their way, you can ask them for access to a list of the wholesalers they are currently working with. Repeat this process with a few of the popular manufacturers in your niche, and you'll begin to see a pattern. Many of the same wholesalers will appear on these lists, and that's a great sign that they're worth giving a call.

• Google. Much like the rule of thumb where a bad website does not mean a bad wholesaler, it's simply the case that for whatever reason, wholesalers are a bit behind on online sales and presence. You'd expect Google to pull up a bunch of wholesalers in a tidy, safe list, but due to their poor website designs and search engine optimization, you may actually have to dig through several pages of Google results. Even once you've found some wholesalers you're interested in working with, you'll need to go through the research required to determine that they are indeed a legitimate resource for you.

• The competition! Finding out the suppliers your competition use may be the easiest way to meet your market's needs. It can be a difficult process to determine which of your competitor's is a dropshipper as well, but when you happen to find one that you believe is a dropshipper, it is easy to order a smaller package from them and take the name off the package if the supplier isn't using their business' name for them. So the address and name on the package will most likely be their supplier, and you can reach out to them specifically in hopes of gaining access to the great products the neighbor was selling.T

• Wholesale directories. Directories of wholesale and discount websites are nothing new, and the unfortunate truth is that many of them do not put in a great effort to determine if an offer is a scam or a fair deal. The great thing is that are a number of wholesale directories that are better than others. These include:

o http://worldwidebrands.com

o http://salehoo.com

o http://doba.com

• Trade shows! One extremely excellent way to find new suppliers is to network with those in your niche or closely related niches. Taking the time to visit trade shows may be a great learning experience, and more importantly, if you ask around about wholesalers and suppliers, you are most likely going to find some great information that a novice may otherwise never learn. Learning from the experiences of others is a brilliant way to move forward. Having relationships with others in similar niches is a great way to get great leads as well.

Before Making the Call

There are some important things you should consider before jumping into a conversation with a potential supplier. So pump the breaks and take a few minutes to consider the following:

• Make sure your business is registered. Wholesalers need as much proof that you're legitimate as possible to spend time on you.

• Remember you're new. Don't start trying to ask for steep discounts just yet. Prove your worth, and you'll be rewarded for this later.

• Setup your store first as a means to help encourage suppliers to work with you.

• Open a business-only bank account. While this isn't necessarily a requirement, it will make your life much easier as time goes on, and if anything should happen where a supplier overcharges, it won't take away from your rent money.

Contacting Suppliers

After you've found your suppliers and done as much as possible to establish yourself as a legitimate business, it is finally time to start reaching out and making contact with them. This process can be a bit daunting for a first-timer, but it will get easier with time, especially as your business becomes more established and your relationships grow with your suppliers. When determining the best way to contact a supplier, the best thing to do first is to scour their website and attempt to determine their preferred contact method. Some will allow for calls or emails, but some prefer one or the other only. It is preferable to find suppliers that are open to emails and email orders, as this will greatly simplify the process of working together later on. Some may require initial contact over the phone but still allow you to place orders through email. If you're ever in doubt, it's probably best to start with a phone call.

Over the Phone

While it may be preferable for you to contact a supplier over email, the truth of the matter is that phone calls tend to offer the most information and helps start a direct relationship with suppliers. If you're the type that doesn't enjoy phone calls and tends to be stressed out during them, especially in new situations, then take time beforehand to write down all of the questions you may have, read them over several times, and keep your notes on hand. It is always wise to have a notebook on hand so you can take notes as well. Swallow the fear, and make the call. Worst case scenario is that they say, "No thanks."

Over Email

When contacting a supplier over email, it is important to include all pertinent information in your correspondence, take the time to proofread your message, and always make sure to offer them a phone number to call you. Much like phone calls, it's wise to take the time to determine exactly what information you would like to have. With emails, the more concise and to the point you can remain, the better information you are likely to receive. Long, winding emails may mean that some of your questions or concerns are not addressed. This method may be much slower as you have new questions once you receive a response.

In Person

While this won't often be the case, if you're attending a trade show and know that there are potential dropshipping suppliers in attendance, it is always possible to meet in person to begin the process. You will very likely need to follow up with email and phone calls, but starting off face to face is a great way to begin that personal relationship that can eventually lead to better prices, star treatment, and a trusting supplier.

What to Ask?

Of course, contacting a supplier without being prepared is going to net poor results. If you're lucky, they'll be happy to receive your call and do their best to be helpful. But just in case you're not sure what you should be asking or the supplier is less-than-helpful in the process, consider the below questions:

• Do you offer a dropshipping program for online sellers? This question can be important for a few reasons. While many suppliers will gladly ship to anyone you want, those that offer a specific dropshipping program are much more likely to place your business name on the shipping label, which helps hide the fact that you're not selling a product you physically store in your own warehouse. This also gives you a chance to clarify that you're not interested in ordering hundreds of a product at once. If there seems to be any confusion, define what you mean by dropshipping.

• Do you offer discounted rates for dropshippers? This can be an important question. While you shouldn't try bartering too much with suppliers you're first contacting, learning about how much they charge is important. The truth of the matter is that many wholesale suppliers are going to charge you a bit more per unit than they would should you be purchasing in bulk. If you happen to work with a retail dropshipping supplier, you'll probably get a decent discount from the retail price, but it may still be too high to justify the time involved in making a sale.

• How do you handle returns and damaged items? This question is CRITICAL. If you don't know how returns work with your suppliers, then you won't know how to handle the customer service part of your business. Understanding these processes upfront is a huge asset to making sure customers are as happy as possible even when things are not going as planned. With damaged items, they should hopefully allow for replacements to be shipped. The more open of a policy they have towards replacing damaged items, the better your peace of mind will be should something arise. In regards to returns made because the customer no longer wants the item, it's important to note that your supplier may only offer a limited returns period. If the return period you offer lasts longer than the duration they offer, you may have to eat the cost of a restocking fee. It is fairly common to see restocking fees as high as 25%, meaning that a $100 item that a customer returns past the date of the supplier's return policy is going to cost you $25. You'll have nothing to show for it, as they'll also get their money back from you. It's a loss, and there's nothing you can really do besides bite the bullet. Keep in mind that one key to a successful ecommerce business is accommodating the customer even when it may hurt your bottom line a bit.

• May I use your images for my product descriptions without worrying about usage rights? You can also ask if their product description is allowed to be used freely, but keep in mind that this is a major faux pas. You should always be generating your own unique content even if it essentially offers the same exact information.

For those products you have decided not to purchase and test (it's ideal to purchase and test when you can, but high-dollar items may not be worth the costs), having their images to use for your product listings is essential to showing the customer what they're buying. If the supplier doesn't allow you to use this content, it's best to move on. Even if you did want to reuse their content, it's likely not going to be optimized for great SEO, and even if it were, the fact that it already exists on the internet is going to ding your ratings on Google. Likewise, most wholesalers aren't in the business of selling retail, so their descriptions probably aren't that sales-worthy anyway.

• How do you accept orders? Find out if they offer email orders, phone orders, have an ordering form, or allow some type of integration system that helps to automate the process. Understanding how they take orders before you make any sales will streamline the process.

• How are your shipping and processing times? If a supplier takes long amounts of time to ship items, it may be best to avoid them. The ideal situation is that your supplier will ship all orders within a few days of receiving payment. Think of this from the perspective of a customer in the 21st century, especially now that Amazon Prime's two-day shipping exists! Customers aren't keen on waiting around for something to ship. While this may be unavoidable in some cases, the more you can minimize the time it takes an item to reach a customer, they happier they'll be.

• Do you provide tracking numbers, and do you provide shipping options? This is another shipping question that's pivotal to the way you advertise your services and shipping. You cannot offer expedited, priority, or economy shipping if your dropshipper only ships with one method. Asking about tracking numbers is also important; customers want a tracking number, especially if the item isn't going to reach them extremely quickly. Most suppliers will offer a tracking number and order confirmation, but it's worth making sure before you commit to conducting business with them.

• Do you produce your own products? This question isn't going to help you decide if you want to work with a supplier or not, but it may give you an idea of how much wiggle room there is to eventually get a better price later on. If a supplier is also the manufacturer and you continue to bring them good business, asking for favors is a lot easier since they aren't losing as much money as a wholesaler or retailer that's purchased the products from a manufacturer themselves.

Keep in mind that they may have a lot of questions of their own, and the more legitimate your business is, the more likely they are to work with you. In the event that a supplier doesn't want to work with you, the only option is to move on. You may approach them again at a later date once you've found other suppliers and have something to show them in terms of sales and website traffic. For those suppliers that require initial orders of a certain amount, the only thing you can offer is to send them the money as a credit and deduct from this credit as you place orders until you're exhausted the balance. If a supplier isn't interested in this, it is again best to simply move on. There are a lot of suppliers out there that are more willing to work with you.

Paying Your Supplier

Suppliers will likely lay out your payment options, and it may vary a bit from one supplier to the next, but generally speaking the payment methods are going to be credit card, wire transfers, and checks. Some suppliers will allow you to simply pay as you go, meaning that as an item is bought, it is charged to your credit card, and then you don't have to worry about it. Others will allow you to pay at the end of the month, especially once the relationship is established, which may be better for your accounting and helps declutter your statements. If you're good at managing money, an end-of-month payment is probably ideal, but the reverse is true if you tend to lose track of how much you owe and begin investing money back into the company without realizing that you still owe a supplier.

Keep Networking

As you can tell by now, the initial steps in working with suppliers may be one of the most complicated parts of dropshipping outside of driving traffic to your ecommerce store. As with any business, the key is to always continue networking with your suppliers and seeking out new suppliers. The better you can establish relationships, the easier the process will become. As trust is gained, it is also reciprocated in other ways. As I've suggested before, should a supplier not want to work with you, there are always others you can work with!

Chapter 7: Marketing to scale up

Unless you're only using third-party marketplaces, which isn't recommended for those aspiring to make very large incomes with dropshipping, then marketing your dropshipping business is going to become an important part of the equation. How do you reach the target audience for your niche? Furthermore, how do you manage this without completely breaking the bank starting off and maximizing on your investment even if you have plenty of money coming in to justify the cost? While there are a lot of benefits to paid advertisements, the best advertisement is having a platform together in your many interactions online.

Search Engine Optimization

We've mentioned search engines optimization quite a bit, especially in regards to keyword research, and it cannot be stressed enough how important it is to play nice with Google. Ultimately, it is my advice to pay an SEO expert to give your site an once-over and give you a plan of action to improve SEO after you have some content available already.

There are a number of things that Google looks for when trying to rank your website within the search results:

• Create content. Having content is key to Google actually indexing your website. Not only do you need content on your site, but you need this to be original content that is not duplicated from other parts of the internet. The more content, the more Google can index, and the more this is original, the less you're penalized for potential plagiarism.

• Keywords. Google looks for keywords and key phrases for obvious reasons, but how you handle these can matter a lot more than you might think. It is important that you're not overusing keywords in an unnatural way. Use a keyword no more than once per 100-300 words, especially if it's unnatural for it to be used so much in the content.

• Images and videos. With Google, images and video will work with their image/video searches if you've utilized them well. This can create an added method of people finding your site, and that also helps your site itself go higher in the page rankings for search results.

• Backlinks. A backlink is any link to another website. The more reputable and higher in the page ranking for

Google the sites that link your page, the better these help you reach higher into the page rankings as well. There is a lot of confusion about backlinks and people will very often have links blasted out to any websites possible. This process is sometimes detrimental to your website, as cheap services for this will often rely on old styles of SEO that no longer apply and end up putting your website links on sites that aren't helping you at all. It is wise to only gain organic backlinks or at least work with a SEO professional.

• Technical stuff matters. The great thing here is that Shopify has their technical aspects together. If your online store is not with Shopify, you will really need to hire a SEO specialist that knows about web design to help you determine if there are any poorly coded portions of your website that need to be updated to allow for the best overall experience for the user and search engine optimization.

There is a lot more to SEO than just understanding these terms and utilizing them, but the general thing to take from this section is that you need original, high-quality content that utilizes images, videos (if possible), and is highly compatible with various web browsers and operating systems. SEO is an organic way to drive traffic, but it is more of a long game than paid advertisements.

Blogging

Adding a blog to your operations is a great way to help add a lot of content to your website, host product reviews, and engage with your demographic. Blogging is an excellent place to utilize SEO, and it gives customers a personality behind the company if done well. The approach you take to blogging can vary. Some will post several times a week, some post only once a week, but the key here is consistency. It makes sense to have a publishing schedule, or it is all too easy to not publish anything at all.

Establishing a blog within your niche that is an authority on related topics is a great way to draw people into your website and thus into your store. It gives you a chance to offer people value even before you ask them to buy anything directly, and it allows you introduce yourself into the community. For a niche that you're not truly familiar with, or if you're a shoddy writer, or if you simply can't make the time, you can always hire a contractor to help write your blog posts. My advice here is to find one that provides an intermediate price for great writing and has some personality that can be interjecting into all the posts. If not using a single writer, then the ideal situation is having a single editor instead, but a very good blogger for hire may not even require much editing, so it's worth paying a little more to avoid low quality content.

Social Media

Social media is almost a requirement for businesses these days, and you would be foolish as a niche store owner not to utilize social media in some manners. The ideal situation is that you will be able to integrate into the online community for your target audiences, either by joining it or working to create a place for them. Creating a place for them, such as a Facebook group, may be the better option, especially if you're great at engaging people over the internet.

Not only does this help you gain some insight into your demographic and feedback on your business, but it also helps establish you as someone that cares within the community, should that apply. This can be a lot of work, but slow and steady is the secret to making it function largely on its own. Like other platforms, you can always hire a contractor to help with this.

At the end of the day, you have to remember that content is king. You cannot simply spam and make snarky comments and expect too much in return. You need to help to provide value first and foremost, and then you can promote your business.

Email List

Having a mailing list helps to send out messages to customers that were willing to sign up for a mailing list, and it has long been touted as one of the most popular ways to gain and keep an audience online. You can promote your mailing list on your blog, on your store page, and of course on social media. The easiest way to gain mailing list subscribers is to offer them some type of value. This can be a coupon code, a free eBook, exclusive deals and content, etc.

Handling your mailing list is best done through services like ConstantContact or MailChimp.com, which are not going to be free, but are much more powerful than attempting to copy and paste a ton of email addresses into your Gmail account.

Product Reviews

Product reviews can make or break a sale. Allowing these on your ecommerce store and making sure to stock great products is a key way to encourage customers to help do the selling for you. Just remember that it is not savory to pay for fake reviews.

Paid Advertisement

Perhaps the easiest and often most effective way of advertising is paying for ad placements within search results, social media, and on other websites. This can be an expensive route to go, but a well-crafted ad campaign can often bring in traffic you simply cannot gain from other methods. Paid advertisements deserve a book to themselves in their complexity, and if the money is there, paying a marketing expert to help with these may actually be cheaper than trying to guess and check on your own.

The number one method for creating a good ad campaign is to create several ads and compare them to one another. The ones with better results get tweaked further and tested again. This is often referred to as "A/B Testing." These ads may only be slightly different from one another, but the results will speak for themselves.

The most common advertising services to use are Google AdWords and Facebook Ads. Obviously Facebook Ads places ads in front of people in social media context, and in many ways this is a great benefit because it is easier to target people that have listed specific interests, ages, and other demographic information. Google AdWords can propagate your ads across search results on the world's largest website, and it also places ads for you on other websites that are relevant to your content and products.

Outside of these two ad services, there are others that are widely ignored by the less experienced. This includes most notably Bing Ads, which works to place your advertisements on search results for both Bing and Yahoo, as well as websites like Google Adwords does. While the direct reach may be less than more popular methods, the cost per click or cost per results are much lower in many instances.

Those keywords that you have learned about along the way are going to be of great use during setting up paid advertisements. With the Google Keyword Planner, the level of competition and the average cost per click is given to you directly for these keywords, helping you understand how the search volume and your placement within those search results is going to help you gain exposure.

There are many other paid advertisement methods worth looking into as well, and ultimately, as long as you're striving for high-quality content, great products, and a pleasant user experience, advertising your entire store or specific products through this method is the fastest way to see results. If your sales content is sales-worthy, it will be greatly worthwhile to invest in advertisements.

Don't Spam

The one major lesson you must understand is that spam does not usually make sales, and it's technically illegal to attempt to be disingenuous with your marketing efforts. Posting comments on every Facebook post isn't going to drive that much business. Posting in forums only to promote a store isn't usually going to work either. If you're going to use these routes for promotion, you need to truly be involved and engaged with those in the community that constitutes your market.

While there is a lot more to marketing than these general overviews, this is going to set you up for putting together a marketing plan that will work for your budget, your target audience, and your goals. I do not suggest relying too heavily on only paid advertisements, just like I don't suggest only focusing on SEO. A well-rounded approach to marketing and engaging the consumer is the best way to move forward.

Chapter 8: Scaling up

Once the drop shipping business has been established, and the owner has a handle on the day to day operations, it will only become a matter of time before the company begins to take off, and in the event this happens, it becomes time to scale upwards. While scaling upwards can be exhilarating and exciting, there are a lot of things that have to be remembered. One key point about scaling is that it does not mean that putting in more hours will result in a linear increase in profits, but rather designing operations in such a way that the sales numbers go up with a lower input of time, though this will require an efficient allocation of resources to get this to happen. Contrary to what a lot of people think, scaling does not necessarily always mean bringing in new people in order to work on or for the business, but doing so is a natural step in the scaling progression. Finding more people to work with you on your brand can be difficult, but if the right people are found who share the same drive and passion, it can be a greatly rewarding step in the scaling process.

In order to begin scaling upwards, the first order of business is to draw a list of tasks that are necessary to the day – to - day operations of the business, and identify which tasks can be outsourced or automated, and which tasks need specific approaches. This list will serve as the basis for your re – allocation of resources, as you can outsource the less important tasks to employees or have them automated entirely, and you can then devote more time to developing business strategies, marketing plans, and working on your rapport with your suppliers

Hiring an Assistant

When you hire an assistant, there are some things that you have to consider. Remembering that one of the perks of having a drop shipping business is that it is relatively location independent, you have two choices. You can hire someone that you know and work together at the same location, such as in an office, a co-working space, a coffee shop, or even at home, or you can hire someone called a VA – a virtual assistant. A virtual assistant is someone you hire over the internet and does not have to be in the same city, country, or even continent as you are in order to do their job, as long as they have access to a stable internet connection, a laptop, and in some cases a phone. Once they have these basic pieces of equipment, provided that you are able to communicate with them in the language you run your business in, that should be enough for the virtual assistant to function. The advantage of hiring a virtual assistant in addition to maintaining location independence is that hiring a VA can be much cheaper than hiring an assistant to work with you where you are, depending on your location. Virtual assistants who live in Eastern Europe or Asia usually have far lower rates per hour as compared to conventional assistants.

Regardless of what kind of assistant you end up hiring, there are a few responsibilities and tasks that can be easily outsourced to them:

1) Social media Handling and Management

2) Customer service and support

3) Graphic design

4) Website maintenance

5) Inventory and order management

6) Content creation / Copywriting

When hiring new people, it is best to create a process flow and a job description for each position in order to make sure that everyone you hire is on the same page when it comes to how you want your business to be run. Hiring a virtual assistant can be as easy as posting on various job sites for freelancers and digital workers such as Upwork, where there are many skilled and qualified freelancers ready and willing to work. The retailer just has to make sure that the process flow and job description is clear, in order that people who apply will have a clear understanding of what exactly the job will entail, and this will help avoid confusion and reduce the likelihood of wasted time.

When picking a virtual assistant, it would be good to conduct an interview over a VOIP platform such as Skype in order to build rapport and to be able to get a better read on the person. It is important to evaluate their application thoroughly, as you will most likely be working closely with them and entrusting them with a lot of responsibility. Even if someone already looks like the perfect candidate, keep a few people in mind as backup in case the first choice doesn't turn out the way you want it to. This is better facilitated if you explicitly tell them that you are hiring them on a probationary basis, perhaps over a period of one month, in order to see how they work.

Remember that while you still have to train your assistant, that training can go both ways, as your assistant may have a lot to teach you as well, based on their previous experience in the industry, or even by applying relevant things that they picked up from working in another industry. The retailer should provide tools for the assistant to learn as well, such as this guide, or other guides that they may deem useful, along with video materials, and once the assistant has gone through it, they can discuss with the retailer their ideas and how they feel that they can be implemented. Training an assistant will usually take about a week, though of course they will learn more while on the job itself. Make sure to keep open lines of communication and be ready and willing to give and receive criticism and feedback in order to create a healthy working relationship.

Scaling through multiple channels

As the drop shipping platform grows, there are a lot of options available in order to scale upwards and access a larger market and increase the sales numbers. One way would be to sell through many different channels such as Amazon, eBay, Oberlo, and other well – established and popular online platforms which will increase the reach of your business. However, there may be issues with this in certain scenarios such as when the same product from a supplier is listed on different sites, and the supplier runs out. Due to the difficulty in keeping the stock count up to date on all sites, this scenario is actually likely to occur. When this happens, backlogs will begin to pile up and product shipments can become delayed, and the customers will begin to be dissatisfied with the service and this may end up being a negative thing for the business. However, this can be worked through or even avoided, especially by getting an assistant to help keep track of the different channels, as well as investing in an inventory management software to be able to track what products are selling and how much stock the supplier has left, in order that the websites can be updated in near – to – real time.

Chapter 9: Personal Branding

During the early days of your business, you are likely going to always feel strapped for resources. As such, it is important to focus first on creating a brand for your company as a whole, before worrying about creating distinctive brands for various lines of products. Assuming the initial brand goes well, you will have plenty of time to create distinctive product lines after the fact. In fact, depending on the type of business you are starting, there may not ever really be a need for sub-branding.

A good brand is the sum total of the way your company looks and feels and also determines who it speaks too and thus who your customer base is going to be. Regardless of the type of business, you are planning on starting, your brand identity should be given serious thought. While the specifics of what constitutes brand identity can be a bit vague, for the purposes of this chapter you can assume it includes graphics and visual presentation, design, iconography, typography, color palette and logo. There are certainly other elements you can include in this list, but these should be enough to get you moving in the right direction.

Think hard about your target audience: When it comes to building a brand, the first thing you are going to want to do is to determine who your target audience is going to be. This is largely going to be influenced by the niche you've chosen, as well as the items that you have your eye on selling. When determining who your target audience is going to be, you are going to want to start by taking to social media and seeing what sorts of people are talking about the products you are thinking about selling.

It is important to really do your research during this step as you want to identify as many interconnected characteristics that you can target amongst those most likely to buy your products for the best results. If you are already a part of this group, then even better, if not, once you have a clear idea of who you are targeting, you are going to want to find out everything about them. This means the types of products they enjoy and what their buying habits are, but also what type of design tends to appeal to their demographic and what their thoughts and values are more likely to be.

If your target audience is under the age of 40, a good way to do this is to go to YouTube and see what type of content is being produced that is related to your target niche. This will give you a good idea of what type of tone is likely to appeal to your target audience and also what type of phrasing and slang to use in your branding.

Choosing a name: While it doesn't take much to pick out a bad company name when you see it, understand what it takes to create a good name can be much more complicated. To get started, you may want to consider which of the three primary name conventions, whimsical, evocative or descriptive, that you want to explore more fully. Descriptive names are self-explanatory, much like the names themselves and include things like Office Depot, Bed, Bath and Beyond and Home Depot. Alternately you can go with something that is evocative without really being descriptive such as Warby Parker or Oracle. Finally, you may want to consider something that's catchy without being meaningful such as Twitter, Google or Hulu.

Colors and fonts: When it comes to choosing the colors and fonts that will help to define your brand, it is important to look professional, even if your target audience typically prefers a more laid back vibe. Presenting a professional product will go a long way towards helping customers trust you, which is going to be one of the biggest initial hurdles you need to surmount with a private label product. When it comes to choosing the right font for your labels it is important to pick something that is easy to read at any size, while still being unique enough to stand out from more traditional selections.

When it comes to finding the right colors to define your brand it is important to choose carefully with the idea that these colors are likely going to be around for quite some time if everything goes according to plan. Additionally, you will want to pick colors that go with the tone or theme of the items you are selling, or something that is of special relevance to the niche in question. Don't forget, different colors mean different things in different niches.

In general, brown is considered a reassuring color that indicates you are confident in your product line. Orange is often associated with energy as well as passion, warmth, originality and starting fresh. When it is paired with blue, current studies suggest that it makes customers think the related product is new and exciting.

Yellow is a color that is best used in moderation as too much can spoil a customer's mood. When used properly, however, it is proven to garner extra attention from customers who see it as playful instead. Green is another color that is generally positive, it is believed to generate feelings of relaxation, safety, harmony, and positivity. Blue is a color that is often associated with being productive as well as peaceful and thoughtful.

The color violet is often associated with the ideals of quality, truth, authenticity, luxury, and spiritual awareness. It is known to create feelings of meditation or contemplation amongst customers. It is also the color most closely associated with royalty, with its color denoting such for more than a thousand years. The color pink, along with the color red cause physical reactions and while red reactions can be strong, pink reactions are more moderate. They include things like love, femininity, warmth, and tranquility. Oddly enough, less than 200 years ago, pink was considered an extremely masculine color because of its connotations with virility.

The color grey is the only common color that has no noticeably physiological results. This makes it inherently a suppressive color and one that should be avoided in high concentrations for the best results. The color black is an intensive color and one that conjures up images of barriers and shrouds. It can also be used to call attention to the stark facts of a situation, making it appropriate in some instance for use in branding purposes.

Consider what your company stands for: Once you have an idea of who your target audience is and what colors you are going to use to connect with them, fleshing out the values and the mission statement of your brand will make the logo creation process discussed below much easier. When it comes to determining the values and the mission statement that is right for your business, it is important to consider the purpose of your company and how that purpose can be seen as inspiring for your customers. Your mission statement should include a clear statement of the values that you hold in the highest regard and how you plan to conduct business both in terms of day to day operations and in a more general sense.

It is also important to point out the character that your business is going to embody as well as any other personal or business standards that you feel are important to your target audience. This is your chance to explain just what sets you apart from the competition, make it count. While making promises to your customers can seem like a great way to flesh out your mission statement, in reality, it is important to limit the number of promises you make, as promising too much can make it difficult to grow in specific ways in the future. Avoid limiting future growth, minimize the guarantees and maximize the generalities for the best results.

If you are having trouble coming up with a mission statement, you may find it helpful to start by first thinking about the products you will be selling and what need they are going to fill. This need is the purpose that your store was created to fill which means it is a great stepping stone to fleshing out your mission statement more thoroughly.

Create a logo

When it comes to creating a successful logo, the first thing you will need to keep in mind is just how omnipresent that it is going to be. In addition to being on all of your products, it is going to be on all of your email correspondence as well as on any advertising that you might want to pay for down the line. This means that the most important consideration of all is always going to be picking something that is malleable enough to expand or contract as needed. After that, consider the colors and fonts that will speak to your target audience most directly.

A perfect logo is one that can be immediately linked to a specific brand, and the company that sells it. When it is created with the right amount of care, a good logo can represent the values and mission statement of your business as well, all with just a single look. If a picture is worth a thousand words, a good logo is worth a thousand conversions, but only if it is done properly. In many cases, a great place to start is a common symbol that potential customers are likely to encounter in their daily interactions as well as on your labels.

If your marketing is successful then your target audience will think of your brand whenever that symbol presents itself, essentially hijacking any other purpose that symbol might have. If you don't think that is likely, consider #. Did you think of that as the phrase "pound key" or did you simply see a hashtag? Twitter took # and if you claim a symbol of your own your target audience won't be able to get away from your brand even if you try.

Additionally, you are going to want a logo that is bold as well as vibrant in such a way that it is sure to catch the eye of any potential customers when they see it as part of your marketing campaign. It also needs to be both clear and visually simple enough for potential customers to instantly have an idea of what they are looking at so they can absorb your branding instead of scratching their heads over just what it is they are looking at.

Your logo is going to be the seal of quality that your diehard customers are going to associate with all the quality that you put into the product acquisition phase. The logo you choose is going to represent your brand for years to come, as changing logos frequently completely negates the point of having a logo in the first place. This means you are going to want to choose something that feels timeless, rather than something that calls out a current moment in the cultural zeitgeist.

This means something that is simple and understated while at the same time unique enough that customers relate it to your company and your company alone. While having a reference in your logo might help you gain a few extra customers in the short term, it will quickly make your company look dated and unwilling to get with the times and is never recommended unless you are only making a single run of a private label product and you don't need to worry about longevity.

Additionally, it is important to avoid using a picture for your logo for a number of reasons. First, they are hard to transition to any other colors besides black and white and, what's more, they are likely going to be in a file format that means they will be difficult to resize properly. What' s more, choosing a stock photo, instead of deciding on something more original, opens you up to numerous other concerns including the fact that if your brand becomes popular, it will be easy for other people to come along and take advantage of your success.

It is important to design your logo around the goal of evoking a specific emotion which means considering the color of your logo as well as any other connotations that facets of it might have to your target audience in order to achieve the best results. Remember, a good logo isn't something you can bang out in an afternoon, it is going to take plenty of trial and error and multiple revisions before it is just right. Slow and steady wins the race.

Chapter 10: Exit Strategies

Every business, even an e-commerce business, needs a solid exit strategy. There are two reasons why you would need to use your exit strategy: either you are not earning enough, or you do not want to keep the business and therefore you want to sell it. Regardless of your reason, having a strong exit strategy in place will ensure that you are prepared for when that time comes.

Exit strategies are simple to create and should be reviewed regularly. Make sure that you are well aware of the terms that surround your exit strategy so that you can be prepared for when your business hits the point where you are ready to make an exit. While it may not come for many years, maybe not even in your lifetime if you choose to pass the business down, having the exit strategy in place and regularly reviewing it is important.

Close Down or Sell

If you are running a business that is not thriving, it may be time to deploy an exit strategy that allows you to shut down your business. While in some cases you can simply shut down shop, in others you may still need to have orders fulfilled and inform existing customers of your impending close. Make sure that you are closing down shop effectively if you are going to do so. You never want to leave your customers hanging because this can lead to you having a difficult time launching a new business and gaining trust in the future. Yes, just because you close down one store does not mean you can't open up a new one in the future.

If you are running a business that is successful or better yet, thriving, then you will want to consider selling your business. This way, you don't take a loss or simply have the income stop flowing. Instead, you can sell your business to someone else who desires to keep it running and you can earn a profit from the effort you put into building your business and getting it to the level where it is now. If you want to sell your business as an exit strategy, it could be because you are not interested in staying in business, because you are looking to make a change in career, because this was the plan all along, or because it has reached a point where you are no longer interested in keeping it going. Regardless of what your own reason will be, you should do your best to identify it early on and create a strategy around that plan.

Business Appraisals

Before you sell your business,ch you need to appraise it. There are many things that go into the appraisal of your business. You may want to consider hiring a professional appraiser to help you with this process as they will be able to give you the most accurate value of your business. The appraisal is more than just knowing how much gross revenue and profit you earn from your business each year. It also factors in the amount of potential growth that can be expected and the strength of the foundation upon which the business was built on.

Before you sell your business, you will always want to appraise it. This will allow you to know what your value is worth. Knowing the true worth of your business means that you can negotiate more effectively and accept offers that are actually reasonable to the value of your business. If you don't know this number, you shouldn't be selling your business just yet.

The Selling Process

Selling a business can be difficult. Just because the business has a certain value does not mean that you are going to get that value from a potential buyer. In fact, you may not get any offers for the first while. In other cases, you may sell the business almost immediately for asking price. For your best interest, you should go into the process with the expectations that you are going to have to be patient and wait for a seller. This keeps you from having to rush and jump on any low baller offer that is tossed your way.

Many people are looking for "turn-key" businesses or businesses which they can buy and maintain as they already are and simply earn the profit from. They do not want to have to invest a significant amount of work into earning their profit, at least not initially. They simply want to step into the driver's seat and expand their business as rapidly as possible without having to put any work into the foundation. The more established your business already is, the more opportunity you will have to sell it to potential buyers.

You should be prepared to negotiate with your potential buyers. There is a good chance that they will come to you with a low offer. If they do, you need to know what the value of your business is and know what you are willing to settle for at your lowest amount. Still, you want to negotiate to bring their number up to as close to the valuation as possible. The more valuable your business is, the more negotiation will need to happen as this is when more complex deals come into play.

Something that most businesses offer which you should be prepared to offer as well is a limited amount of ongoing support. You should be prepared to offer the buyer at least 30 days of support with email systems and guidance so that they can learn to seamlessly take over the company. This gives them the opportunity to have a smoother take over instead of them stepping in and not being clear on how you have run your company until this point. It also assists with the sale process as people like knowing that they will be guided to take over your success instead of plopped into the seat of a car they don't know how to drive.

Remember, just because you reach the negotiation process with a certain potential buyer doesn't mean you are going to make a sale. You might negotiate with many potential buyers before you reach a deal that actually meets your needs for your business. Don't feel obligated to make a sale just because you have entered the negotiation phase with a potential buyer. In fact, reaching this stage and leaving it if the clauses aren't promising for yourself as the seller can work in your favor. In some cases, when a buyer is particularly motivated, threatening to reject the deal altogether can encourage them to come closer to your desired value. It shows them that you have decided what you want for the business and that you are not willing to sell for any less. It also shows that your company is actually valuable because you aren't willing to sell it off for any ballpark number.

When to Sell?

As aforementioned, you will likely have your own reason as to why you are going in business. If you are going into business with the intention to build a six figure business, you likely want to keep your business running until you no longer desire to run it. However, you may also want to sell it when it reaches a certain valuation so that you can walk away with a lump sum from the business.

When you decide to sell your business will largely depend on what your intention with the business is. Once you have decided what will trigger the sale, then you need to pick the perfect time to actually get into the market and sell your business.

The first thing you need to consider is the state of your business. A company that is on an upward trend for gaining profit and traffic is one that will have greater sales potential and a higher valuation. People want a business that is growing, not one that has reached its peak or is beginning to dwindle. When your business is in a state of thriving, it is a good time to consider entering the market for the sale of your business.

Another thing to consider is the state of the current market. While businesses will almost always sell well, a recessed market may result in you having to settle for less than your business is worth just to make the sale. If you are not willing to take the hit on your sale price you will want to wait until the economy comes back up so that you can earn your desired value from your business.

Once your business and the market are in the right position, you can consider selling your business off. This will provide you with the opportunity to earn a large amount of capital off of it which you can invest elsewhere. With that money, you may consider starting a new business venture or investing in one that you are already operating so that you can grow it significantly. That is completely up to you.

Having a strong exit strategy in place for your business is extremely important. Any business, even one that is anticipated to stay in business for a long period of time, needs to have an exit strategy. There are many reasons as to why you may want to exit your business and having this strategy in place can give you the opportunity to make an efficient exit that will not damage your success or profits. Make sure that when you are in the process of creating your business plan that you also create an effective exit strategy that will allow you to exit the market properly when you are ready to. An improper exit strategy can lead to you selling prematurely, losing money, or otherwise running into a rookie mistake with your exit strategy.

Chapter 11: Practical Tips and Lessons from Successful Dropshippers

Tips and tricks are always great for anything new that you are learning - it makes us able to accomplish things better, more efficiently, in less time and achieve better results. Here are eight tips to master your online dropshipping business:

1 - Keep Your Eye on the Ball

Your main goal is to create profits, so that should be your focus. Do not get carried away by flashy graphics and so called 'must-haves' for your website or even long content that apparently 'speaks' to your audience. You do not want to lengthen the time it takes for your customers to decide to purchase your product.

The idea is to get them to your site, browse for what they want, click on the product, read a short description and buy it. Keep things moving forward and avoid anything that detracts you from this mission.

2 - Think Like a Customer

One of the reasons why you need to stick to a niche that you know and one that you are passionate about is, so you understand customer pain points.

What do you look for when you are on someone's website? What do you expect to find there? What kind of buying process makes you feel you purchase things fast? What makes you like the website you usually purchase from?

Knowing the pain points yourself makes you understand what your customers want and how your product can help them accomplish their needs.

3 - SEO Your Site

Part of your marketing should also be SEO. SEO is not dead so long as keywords are still used to search for anything and everything on the internet. You need to use SEO wisely, not only on your website but also on your social media which is from content, titles, tags, image tags, descriptions- the whole nine yards. You will be found much easier through specific keywords.

4 - Product Reviews

The best way for any customer to know that the products they are purchasing are value for money is by reading reviews. Customers will click on products that have higher ratings and the likelihood of them purchasing it is if it has good and high reviews.

DO NOT cheat on your reviews. If you have a product that always gets bad reviews - trash it. When you do, let your customers know that you are discontinuing it because this will help increase their confidence in your site. The fact that you have heard them, and you are doing something about it increases brand trust.

5 - Mix Your Marketing

There are many ways to reach your customers depending on who they are and what they do. For most dropshipping marketing methods, social media marketing and email marketing is the way to go. But you should not rely on it entirely. It is also good to meet with your customers and see who they are. Host product giveaways, hold online workshops or seminars, have an online meet-and-greet, feature your customers using your product or give them a shout out!

6 - Make Your Logistics Work Well

Have strong and clear agreements on any potential logistical issues that you may encounter in your dropshipping business. Outline these in your contract and have this on your website. Inform customers what to do if they have returned.

Outline this with your supplier as well and establish standard operating procedures for returns, damaged items and so on. Outline what the shipping costs are as well between yourself and the supplier and what is the expected delivery date for your items between supplier and customer.

7 - Establish Your Relationship with Your Supplier

Establishing and maintaining close relationships with your suppliers ensures that you can also extend the benefits to your customers.

When you supplier trusts you, there will be many things that you can get done such as offer personalized packaging to your customers, ensuring speedy shipping and having reduced time in managing any issues you must deal with if there are delays. Collaboration is based on trust and the quicker you establish trust, the better.

8 - Communicate Your Product Strategy

Strong product descriptions ensure higher success rates of purchasing. This information is critical to your customer - they want to know what they are buying and the better you describe your product, the faster it would be for your customers to make a purchasing decision.

Do not give long and vague descriptions and do not put in duplicate content. Duplicate content will be penalized by search engines.

Chapter 12: The Money Mindset

Business and entrepreneurship is always a tough start. Being a successful person is not just what you wake up and become. For you to be the success you really wished for, you have to do what successful people are doing that makes them win. Successful people have a different mindset from every other person, the way they think and do things is always special. In this chapter, I will be taking you through what you have to do to have a winner's mindset.

Before we move on, let us set the right tone and mindset. A dropshipping business model is far from the fantasies of easy money and get rich quick schemes. A dropshipping business, like every other thing in life, requires hard work and dedication combined with knowledge and multiple failures. Never good is ever easy. The biggest victories and greatest rewards never come from the completion of easy tasks.

Mental preparation refers to act of preparing mentally or unlocking the mind to achieve success. It helps in developing concentration and decision making skill. Mental preparation is training the mind for successful performance. Here are some of the elements of mental preparation: mental sturdiness, inspiration, motivation, composure, goal setting, stress management and relaxation. The pressure to be successful increases when going into any business or taking any kind of risk and mental preparation is more important than ever.

Anxiety impedes your decision-making ability, which leads to an imperfect execution, and lowers your performance. **Mental preparation** is key to remaining relaxed and composed under the pressure of been successful. You must be psychologically and mentally prepared to face all the challenges ahead without fear.

Here are some mental preparation tips to keep you performing at your best level;

- Develop a consistent plan that instills confidence. A good plan will help you focus on what you need to do to perform. Taking time before going into business to mentally prepare will create confidence, composure, and relaxed mindset.
- Focus on the process, not results. Focusing on the outcome of the business causes you to think too far ahead and sets too many expectations for the

business. You will start to put too much pressure on yourself which is not healthy for your business.

- Have trust in yourself. Believing in yourself and skill instil confidence in you. You have to perform freely and trust in your skills, it will really help your productivity.

Become mentally prepared by focusing on your goal and all the laid down plans, avoid thinking about results, and trust your preparation and ability.

There is surely going to be many obstacles to achieving financial freedom through passive income, be strong, courageous and never give up. It is important to understand all the obstacles and challenges ahead and be fully prepared so that you can manage them well. Being honest with yourself and keeping your eyes open will increase your chances of success in this business. You should not run away from obstacles, do not try to play it safe and find another way out, confront it with confidence and never give up. You are never defeated until you accept defeat as a reality and stop trying, so you have to keep pushing hard and never lose your focus. Just accept any obstacle that comes as you move on with your business and fight it off with solutions that are extremely creative. The only real limitations on what you can accomplish are those that you impose on yourself. The troubles will come, the challenges will be many and the opposition fierce, but be confident and stay strong, you will come out successful. The dictionary defines courage as the quality of mind enabling one to face danger or hardship resolutely. It is the ability to control fear and to deal with danger, pain and uncertainty. It also means bravery, fearlessness and gallantry. Outstanding success is for strong-hearted men. It takes toughness to taste triumph. Courage — your access to outstanding success!

"Effort only fully releases its reward after a person refuses to quit."

 --Napoleon Hill

Hardwork is the pathway to progress, the means to produce a desired result and it will take you to the top where you belong. The more you apply yourself to hardwork, the better you become. A hard worker presses on in spite of all odds. Success is impossible until your hands are set to work. Diligence is one of the principles for success on the earth, it involves investing your abilities, strength and all you have into the pursuit of your goal. The cheapest way to fight failure is to work hard. There is no substitute for hard work, if you must succeed. Great success will not come your way without great commitment. Committed work toward a desired result is also a key to your success. You have to be persistent in what you're doing because persistency is norm for winners. The driving force behind productivity is diligence, so you have to work diligently for you be highly productive. Without diligence you can accomplish nothing. It is impossible to see success without diligence. Success is not a gift, it is an achievement. It is not imposed on people, it is obtained by proper planning and due diligence. Hardwork is the key to your personal development, output, and achievement. Excellent work always profits the worker.

Planning is the process of making the right decision carefully on how to get things done prior to actually starting to do it. Without making the right decision on how to run our daily business, we will never be able to optimize our productivity. You need to concentrate your time and resources in planning to accomplish your goals.

Making the right decision before starting to do something is never a waste of time. Productivity will increase geometrically and there will be a great reduction in the execution time when sufficient time is spent in planning which will make you more successful.

The lack of discipline is the nemesis of success. For you to be highly successful in this BUSINESS you must be highly disciplined. You need to do the right thing at the right time. You will never find a successful person who is not diligent in all his ways. From the story of great and successful men, you will find out that they are dedicated and diligent worker. Knowledge is not beneficial until it is transformed into Action, everything you're going to learn in this book is going to be a total waste if you did not stand up and act immediately.

"Great achievement is usually born of great sacrifice, and is never the result of selfishness." --Napoleon Hill
Productivity simply means realizing your desired goals and achieving favorable results. If you really want to realize your long term goals, you need to clearly envisage them and do the right things at the right time. People that are highly productive carefully plan well and prioritize their life and their actions towards their business.

To have success, you must choose to have focus. Focus stimulates your desire to be a winner. It's important to remember that focus is an attitude before it becomes an action, and it's a journey more than a destination. Focus demands your discipline to become a winner, and discipline begins with a definite decision by you. Focus also strengthens your determination to become a winner. Your position may never change, until there is that inner force propelling you towards your desired goal. Pursuit is the relevant force that helps bring your long term goal into reality. You should be goal-driven and motivated. The best investment is in your own education. Invest time and money into dropshipping business. Create a timeline and set goals.

"A goal without a timeline is simply a dream."

– Robert Herjavec, Shark Tank Billionaire

If you are a person who requires instant rewards and gratification, this book is not for you. Dropshipping enforces the concept of delayed gratification. In this day and age we are living in a fast paced world. We are constantly bombarded by information that is readily available everywhere. Hence I would understand if the concept of delayed gratification is foreign to you. We touch a switch and the lights instantly appear. We whip out our phones and are able to do wonders with it instantly. Technology has made us crave instant gratification. However with the advancement of technology comes great opportunity. There is BIG MONEY to be made. Execution is way more important than an idea. Online income defines the new rich. Put in the work first, reap the rewards later and FOREVER.

Chapter 13: Frequently asked questions

Who pays the cost of shipping an item to the customer?

Generally, your supplier will use their account with Fed Ex, UPS, or whatever method of shipping they use to pay the shipping and handling fees for your product. This cost will then be added onto the wholesale price that you owe them for the item. You can choose to charge your customers any amount for the shipping cost of the item. Some drop shippers will offer free shipping on their items, charge a flat rate, or calculate the exact cost of the item's shipment to pass on to the customer.

Will the order look like it came directly from my company when it arrives at the customer's location? Usually, it will. Most wholesalers give retailers the option to have labels appear with their information.

What will I do about a customer return?

You'll need to state what items you will and won't accept for return (if any) and what condition they need to be in, or what reasoning you'll need to accept a return. This information should be provided to your customers before they purchase an item, and again before you agree to accept a return from them. If you decide to accept an item as a return from a customer, you'll most likely be given a return authorization number from your supplier that will identify the customer's return. Provide this number as well as the address of the supplier's warehouse or return department to the customer so they can mail the product back. Once they receive the item and process the return, you'll be given credit for the cost you paid for the item, and you can then return the cost (minus any fees you won't be refunding like say, shipping) to the customer.

Where do I find suppliers that I can establish a drop shipping relationship with?

There are services you can use online (usually with a fee associated) that can connect you with companies that routinely supply items and fulfill orders for drop shippers. You can also directly contact the manufacturer of a product you're interested in offering or by spending some time doing in-depth and detailed Google searches for trustworthy suppliers.

How quickly will my customer's orders be fulfilled and shipped out?

This varies depending on the supplier you're using for the order, but a quality wholesaler should be able to ship an order the same day if it's received before noon, and the next day if the order is received later than that.

Conclusions

By reading this book you are more equipped to handle dropshipping than the people who are currently successful dropshippers were when they started. The downside of all this information is that it is possible to enter into the state of paralysis by analysis and to try to perfectly curate the strategy by leveraging other people's mistakes. There is also bound to be a lot of contradicting information which will confuse people even further.

The things that helped me personally learn the most is simply trying and testing things out and seeing what works and what doesn't and the logging everything and perfecting the process like a scientist. When testing things out it is necessary to take just the right amount of risk so that you would see how something works without the chance of being damaged too much. Thankfully, the online businesses of today allow this kind of testing and today it is surprisingly a lot more important to be a good data analyst instead of being the stereotypical marketing expert.